How to Start a Blog

The Ultimate Beginner's Guide to Creating, Marketing, and Monetizing a Successful Blog

The author of this book has taken careful measures to share vital information about the subject. May its readers acquire the right knowledge, wisdom, inspiration, and succeed.

Table of Contents

Introduction

Congratulations on purchasing this book and thank you for doing so.

The following chapters will teach you everything that you need to learn about starting a blog and turning it into a goldmine.

Chapter 1 explains the basics of blogging so that you will have a good foundation and understanding of what blogging and being a successful blogger are all about.

Chapter 2 teaches how you can create a blog, as well as everything that you need to consider when setting up your blog.

Chapter 3 talks about the way to market your blog in order to reach a bigger audience and draw more traffic to your blog.

Chapter 4 shows the different ways to monetize your blog. This is the part where you turn your blog into a money-making machine.

Chapter 5 lays down the best blogging practices observed by highly successful bloggers. You should turn these practices into a habit for they serve as the foundation of every successful blog.

Chapter 6 reveals the pitfalls that beginners often encounter. You should be aware of these pitfalls and make the necessary adjustments so that you can avoid committing the same mistakes.

There are plenty of books on this subject on the market, thanks again for choosing this one! Every effort was made to ensure it is full of as much useful information as possible. Please enjoy!

Chapter 1
The Basics

As human beings, it is in our nature to share. People share their knowledge, expertise, opinions, and even their life's experiences. Some believe that it is this act of sharing (giving and receiving) is the way how the world continues to exist. In today's age that is heavily dominated by computers and ever-rising technology, it is much easier to share anything with the world. People all over the globe are able to share how they feel or think with just a few clicks of a mouse.

When it comes to sharing, blogging has become an effective way to connect with like-minded people. You can try and make some searches on the Internet and you will see countless of blogs appear on search engine result pages. Every blog page that you see always has something to share. In fact, with so many blogs out there and still new blogs being added every day, you can expect to find multiple blogs on any subject that you can think of. This is the beauty of blogging. It is the beauty of sharing.

What is a Blog?

A blog is your personal space in the Internet universe. You are free to write anything that you want on your blog. For example, those who are passionate about business create and manage business blogs, while those who are interested in bodybuilding come up with fitness blogs and share useful information, including their personal experiences. Simply put, your blog is as meaningful as you make it.

Why Blog?

People blog for various reasons. In fact, you do not even need a reason to blog. There are those who blog simply to share what they know with the world, while others do it for money. Yes, you can earn a decent amount of profit with blogging; however, it is not as easy as it seems. If you have something to share, then blogging is an effective way to do it. You can have the whole world as your audience.

Is it for You?

It is true that anyone can blog; however, blogging is not really for everyone. The reason is that to have real success with blogging, you need to put in time, effort, and hard work. The good news is that everyone has something meaningful to share. Every person has a story that only he alone can tell the world. If not an interesting story, then you can also share your expertise or knowledge about something. Of course, if you just want to blog as a hobby where you just update your blog at any time you want and do not exert any effort in promoting it, then you can also do that. However, do not expect for your blog to generate a decent income. If your aim is to create a profitable blog, then you should also give it the time and effort that it deserves. Also, do not forget that you have competitors to deal with.

How Much Money Can You Make?

The money that a blog can make ranges from zero to countless of dollars per month. There are bloggers that only earn pennies with their blogs, while truly successful bloggers are able to quit their day job and work full time on their blog. If you blog for profit, then you should consider it as an investment. And, like any other investment, there are risks involved, and there is a possibility that you may not earn anything worthwhile from it.

Blog vs. Website

This book uses both terms (blog and website) synonymously. However, for the word geeks out there, there are some differences between the two. A blog usually gets updated with new contents on a regular basis, while a website has a more static page and less activity. Interactions and engagements are also common for blogs, while websites do not always have a space for visitors to place their comments or reviews. A blog is like social media but is a bit more formal and made especially for one person (the blogger), while a website is usually more formal than a blog. It is also worth noting that a blog is also a website, but a website is not always considered a blog.

SEO

SEO or Search Engine Optimization is important if you want to have any success with blogging. SEO is the practice of increasing your blog's visibility so that it can easily be located by search engines. Do not forget that for you to draw lots of traffic to your blog, you need search engines like Google to recommend your blog to people via the search engine result pages (SERP). According to a study, around 60% of those who search the Internet does not go beyond the first page of a search result. Therefore, your aim is to place your blog on the first page of Google and other search engines. The way to do this is by applying the best SEO practices.

When it comes to SEO, an important thing to take note of is to produce high-quality contents. Make sure that every article that you publish has a high quality. This means that your posts should be informative enough so that your readers will find them useful. The next thing that you should know is how to use keywords effectively. When people talk about SEO, the use of keywords is something that you cannot miss. It is worth noting that the days are gone when you can just use one or two keywords and still expect search engines to find your site. Today, you need to use a keyword phrase, also known as long-tail keywords. Long-tail keywords are composed of three or more words.

You might be wondering why they are called keywords. They are keywords because they primarily relate to the article, and they are repeated several times in the same article.

Keyword Density

Keyword density refers to the number of times your keywords are repeated in an article. Various webmasters and bloggers have been asked regarding what they think would be the best keyword density, and they have all given different answers.

As it appears, there is no hard and fast rule on how many times you should repeat your keywords in your article. However, it is strongly recommended that you keep the keyword density around 1% to 3%. This is the optimum keyword density rate.

Of course, there are other SEO techniques that you can use, but providing top-quality contents and using keywords effectively are the two main ingredients of a powerful SEO, so be sure to keep these two on your list.

Traits of a Successful Blogger

You might think that success in blogging is easy and simple. After all, all that you need to do is to type whatever you know and hit the publish button on a regular basis. Well, it turns out that becoming a successful blogger is not that simple. There are traits that you need to turn into a habit, which marks the very foundation behind every blogging success.

- You should blog regularly

Unlike a website, a blog should be active, regularly updated with fresh contents. Therefore, you need to strive to blog regularly. Also, you are expected to produce high-quality blog posts all the time. Continue to publish exciting blog posts and keep your readers interested in your blog.

- You should interact with your readers

Your job is not done the moment you publish a blog post. In fact, you are only half way through. So, you have published a new blog post? Then that is good. But, comments from your readers will start rolling in, and you need to answer them — yes, each one of them. It does not matter even if it takes you a week to answer all the comments, but it is important that you do not make your readers feel that they are being ignored. Interacting with your readers is also an effective way to keep them interested in your blog, so consider this as part of your marketing strategy.

- You should proofread your articles

Successful bloggers approach blogging professionally. They do not like low-quality posts. They are also keen to details, such as by observing proper grammar and punctuation. Misspellings are also common, so keep your eyes on them. Make sure that you offer to your readers the best content that you can come up with. You should not let typo errors ruin the beauty of your article.

- You should take advantage of social media

One of the striking characteristics of successful bloggers is that they have a strong presence online, especially on social media. Social media is also a good way to promote your blog. This will be discussed later on in this book. If you want to be like the top bloggers out there who earn a decent amount of income with their blog, it is strongly recommended that you have at least one social media account.

- You should keep yourself updated

You should follow for the latest updates on blogging, such as the best SEO and blogging practices, as well as the pitfalls that you should avoid. Blogging is a lifelong journey. It can be considered as an art form that continuously develops as professional bloggers strive to make their blog better and better.

- You should know the purpose of your blog

Although you may not have a reason or purpose for blogging, your blog itself should have a purpose. This is a good way to define your blog so that people can know what to expect from your blog. Also, if you want to blog for money, then you should observe the best practices to convert visitors into sales. Knowing the purpose of your blog is important so that you can adjust how you approach your blog. If your blog does not have a purpose, then it will also be hard for you to define goals to achieve with your blog. Know the purpose of your blog and work for that purpose.

- You should be open to criticism

When you blog, you open and make yourself vulnerable to criticisms. This is part of blogging just as authors open themselves to be critiqued each time they publish a book out in the market. The same goes when you blog. In fact, it is not uncommon even for successful bloggers to receive negative comments from time to time. You should learn how to handle criticisms properly. Sometimes, the development of your blog may come by understanding your criticisms that you may receive.

- You should focus on giving value

Regardless of the topic of your blog or the niche that you specialize in, the most important part of blogging is giving value to your visitors. Look at the top blogs out there, the reason how they got established is that they continue to give value to their blog visitors. Value, of course, is given through the articles that you publish on your blog. The information that you share with your readers is vital to your success. You also need to compare what you share with the value that your competitors give to the market. Hence, it is important to be unique so that you would not have to make any comparison. Share your own voice with the world, and let your perspectives help the people who read your blog.

- You should enjoy your blog

Yes, you can blog about what you think is the "hot" trend these days and hope to make money out of it. In fact, you can just be a businessman and hire ghostwriters to do all the work for you. But, if you take a look at the most successful bloggers in the world, they are the ones who blog with passion. No matter how you look at it, blogging is about writing and sharing something valuable with the world. How do you expect to share something unique and meaningful if you are not interested in your topic? Also, blogging is a lifelong journey. Successful blogs run for years and years. If you do not have an interest in your subject, then you will also not have the patience to work on your blog. Take note that managing a profitable blog takes time and effort. Also, blogging for profit is a business. As such, there are risks involved, and part of this risk is not earning with your blog despite following all the suggestions and best practices that you can learn. But, if you enjoy your blog, if you like the topic that you are blogging about, then you can always consider your blog a success even at the onset. Hence, blog about something that you love. Enjoy the journey.

- You should share

Blogging is about sharing. As they say, sharing is caring. This is also the way to build trust. And, you should share meaningful things and not just the mere basics that almost everybody knows about your topic. Take note that there are many other blogs in the world that talk about your subject, so you have to share something from a different perspective. To do so, you need to share your own views on the subject. Hence, you need to open your heart and mind and share them with the world. Sharing is the blood of blogging. The moment you cease to share, the blog stops and even the number of your followers may decline. But, the more you share meaningful and valuable things with your blog, the more you get closer to success.

Chapter 2
Create a Blog

It is not the time for you to learn how to create a brand-new blog so that you can start sharing your thoughts and ideas with the world. Creating a blog is easy. Just stick to the steps in this chapter and enjoy the process. After all, blogging should be fun!

Blog Hosting

The first step is for you to decide whether or not you will host your blog. Hosting a blog is about owning a space on the Internet. Now, if you just want to test the water and blog as a hobby, you might want to use free-hosted sites so that you would not have to spend any money. However, if you are serious about making a profit, then it is strongly recommended that you host your own blog.

Have you seen those websites with .blogspot or .wordpress in their URL? That is what happens when you do not host your own blog. When you do not host your own blog, you only get to own a subdomain. The problem here is that you do not have control over your domain. If the main domain encounters a problem and closes down, then it will be a big problem for you. Also, you cannot expect people to treat you seriously if you do not even host your own site. It demonstrates a lack of seriousness and devotion. Do not worry; hosting a site is not expensive. On average, you will only have to spend less than $20 a year to host your own site.

There are many hosting services that you can find online, such as Namecheap, Godaddy, Bluehost, and others. If the blogging platform that you use is WordPress, then you might want to use Bluehost. Why? Well, even WordPress itself promotes Bluehost. Of course, you are still free to try other hosting services.

Domain Name

Be careful in choosing a name for your blog, or more specifically, the domain URL name of your blog. Take note that you cannot change your domain name, so be sure to pick the best one from the start. For SEO purposes, it is suggested that you include a keyword (even just a single word) in your domain name. It may be a generic word that tells what your blog is about so that people will easily get an idea what your blog is just from its name. For example, if it is a travel blog, then it may include the word *travel*.

Blogging Platform

In order to start blogging, you need to use a blogging platform. There are many available platforms that you can use online, such as Blogger, WordPress, Win, and others. Most people recommend WordPress. However, if you want a blogging platform that is very simple to use that you do not need any HTML knowledge, then you might like to use Blogger. Blogger is Google's blogging platform.

Creating Contents

Content creation is the number one element of a blog. To have a successful blog, you need to provide quality contents to your readers. There are two ways to generate contents for your blog: You can create the contents yourself and/or you can hire a ghostwriter to make the contents for you.

Of course, the best way is still for you to be the one to create the contents. After all, it is your blog. Do not worry; you do not need to be a professional ghostwriter to come up with quality posts. However, you may need to learn even just the basic rules of writing. After all, when you blog, it is through your writing that you connect with your audience. Therefore, it is only right that you learn how to write effectively.

There are people who have amazing ideas but are not able to express them properly in writing. A good advice is to study the basic rules of grammar and punctuation, and just keep on writing. The more you write, the easier it will be for you to express yourself in writing. Do not forget that writing is also an art; and, just like any other art, it requires continuous practice so that you can be really good at it. Needless to say, blogging regularly is a good way to develop your writing skills. Just keep in mind that you should only publish posts that are of high quality. Do not hesitate to keep on working on your manuscript until it is of a professional caliber that you can be proud of.

There are also people who simply do not have time to write or have no interest in improving their writing skill. In such case, the solution would be to hire a professional ghostwriter. A ghostwriter is a person who will write your contents for a fee. Take note that he will not claim ownership of the work. You remain as the author of the piece that a ghostwriter writes. It will be a secret between you and your ghostwriter. Hence, people who hire a ghostwriter usually enter into a Non-Disclosure Agreement with their ghostwriter. Now, there are two main things that you should consider when you hire, a ghostwriter: the fee and quality.

Although you can easily find many ghostwriters at content mills online, like Freelancer and Upwork, who would agree to write your blog contents for a cheap price; it is hard to find ghostwriters who can write well. Unfortunately, many of these people who claim to be ghostwriters are far from professionals. They are hacks and scams who have not yet written a single high-quality book. This also explains why they usually agree to write articles for as low as $3 per 500-word article.

When working with ghostwriters, quality and price (fee) often go hand in hand. Professional ghostwriters who write well know the value of their talent and would not accept a project for a low fee. Of course, you can get lucky and find a skilled writer to work with you at a low price, but do not expect him to work for you for a long term. True and professional ghostwriters value their writing because true writing art requires perseverance, dedication, and years of practice.

A word of caution: Just because a ghostwriter charges a high fee does not always mean that he is one of the top ghostwriters out there. Unfortunately, the online world is also full of scams and hacks just like the physical world. Therefore, do not forget to ask for a potential ghostwriter's portfolio, and take note how he responds to your messages. Pay attention to how he structures his messages, as well as the flow of his lines. Just like with any kind of dealing, exercise caution and diligence.

Again, the best way is still for you to be the one to write the contents of your blog. Hiring a true professional ghostwriter can be costly, especially if you intend to hire him for a long term. Also, it is your blog, so it is just right that you exercise full control over it.

Blog Layout and Design

Your blog should have an attractive layout and design that will increase the readability of the contents and give the best user experience. For starters, your blog should have the basic features, which can help your visitors to more easily navigate your blog. These basic features are the following:

- Header

- Search bar

- Pages

- Sidebars (optional)

- Options to subscribe

- Contact page

When you look at the different blog templates and designs that you can use, you may be tempted to use one has many decorations and colors. Although such design may look attractive, it is recommended that you stay away from it. The suggested design is one that is simple yet professional. Do not let your design make your blog look complicated to navigate. Take note that although a blog's design is important, visitors to your blog are more concerned with your contents and not with the design of your blog. Therefore, use your design to highlight your contents and not the other way around.

As for the color of your blog, there are many color combinations that you can use. Some say that you can use any one color of your choice so long as you combine it with a primary color. You can also use the color gray to give your blog a more formal appearance. However, a combination of colors is an art. There is really no right and wrong way to do it. It is only suggested that you use a color combination that will make your blog be more presentable and do not sacrifice the professional appearance of your blog.

Quality vs. Quantity

You should understand the importance of quality and quantity of your posts. Now, many people will tell you that you should focus on the quality. The reason is that merely uploading posts filled with keywords is no longer applicable. Google and other search engines have already developed their algorithm. Today, you can only increase your chances of being on the front page of the SERP if you have high-quality posts. However, simply saying that you should focus on the quality is quite misleading. The thing is that quantity or the number of posts that you publish on your blog is also important. After all, you cannot expect your blog to be recommended by search engines like Google if you only have five articles on your blog, regardless of the quality of your contents. The reason is that search engines will not be able to tell exactly what you site is about simply by using a few posts as a basis. Therefore, just as you need to update your blog with high-quality contents, you should also keep in mind that you should have as many high-quality articles on your blog as possible. This is an effective way to increase your blog's SEO ranking. Hence, although the quality is more important than quantity, quantity is still an element that you cannot ignore.

Chapter 3
Marketing

No matter how informative or wonderful your blog is, it will not be able to generate enough traffic to earn a significant amount of traffic if people are not aware that your blog exists. Therefore, you must put in some marketing efforts to draw attention and interest to your blog. If you do not promote your blog, there is a high probability that it will end up unnoticed among the piles of other blogs in the web. Take note that marketing your blog is an essential element of any successful blog.

Social Media Marketing

When it comes to marketing and promotion, the power of social media cannot be ignored. Social media makes sharing contents fast and easy. There are many social media platforms available. The top social platforms that you should consider are Facebook and Twitter. If you want to rank well on Google search engine, then this book suggests that you also include Google Plus. Google Plus is Google's own social media platform.

It is very easy to spread a word using social media. Another advantage of using social media is that your network or connections can share your content with their own network, so on and so forth. Just imagine how many people you can tap just by utilizing the use of social media. It is also through social media that a blog post can get viral on the Internet. Therefore, if you are serious about having any profitable success with your blog, social media marketing should be on your list.

Social media platforms normally have groups where you can freely discuss something that you are interested in. This is also an effective way to connect with like-minded people. For example, if your blog is about poetry, then you can join poetry groups. If your blog is focused on business, then you can also find many businesses groups that you can join. You can post on the group's page with a link to your blog as a way of promoting your blog. However, do not overdo it, and be sure to know the group's guidelines on posting. Some groups do not like self-serving or promotional posts.

Guest Posting

Guest posting is another effective way to drive traffic to your blog. But, what is guest posting? Guest posting simply means posting an article on another person's blog or website. You also get to keep the byline, so people will know that you are the author of the article. So, how can guest posting help you promote your blog? Most blogs that accept guest posts will allow you to include a short bio and a link to your site. This is how you promote your site. And, what is more, most established blogs pay for guest posts. Hence, not only will you be able to promote your blog, but you can also earn money at the same time. It is not uncommon to find blogs that pay more than $50 for a 500-word article guest post.

Take note that you should aim to guest post on well-established blogs. These blogs have a huge following. Just imagine how much you can benefit if you are able to lead the traffic from that blog to your blog. However, to make those people take interest in checking out your blog, you need to provide them with an interesting and useful article. If you do, then they may be persuaded to find out more about you — and that is by checking out the link that leads to your blog.

It should also be noted that well-established blogs do not just accept any kind of guest post. Normally, you will have to pass the editorial guidelines, and you need to come up with a high-quality article. This usually takes some good level of writing skill. Do not worry; if the blog where you intend to guest post does not accept your article, you can just publish it on your blog. If you really want to guest post and promote your blog and the only hindrance is that you cannot write effectively, then maybe that is the time that you should consider hiring a professional ghostwriter.

How will you know if a blog accepts guest posts? Most of these blogs or sites provide a Write for Us page or editorial guidelines on their blog. Also, if you notice that a particular blog has many authors, then it may be a sign that it accepts guest posts. The best way to find out is to contact the blog's admin via the Contact Us page. You can also make a search online for a list of blogs and websites that accept guest posting. Just be prepared to write a compelling query letter and a high-quality article.

Locked Contents

Another marketing technique is to lock some of the contents on your site. This means that the reader will have to like or share your content on social media before he can even access the whole article. This is a good thing to do, especially if the title and introductory paragraph of your article are strong and persuasive. This will compel your visitor to share your article so that he can read the full text. There are WordPress plugins that you can use to do this, as well as HTML codes that you can apply. Take note that you only lock some articles on your site. Of course, you can decide to lock all your contents but such would not look good to your visitors. Avoid giving the impression that you are in need of getting social media shares or likes. Of course, as always, be sure that your contents are of high-quality.

Some people make a mistake of locking high-quality articles and having all not-so-well-written articles open to the public. The problem here is that once people read your low-quality articles, they will no longer be interested in checking the locked contents of your blog. Instead, they will just leave your blog immediately and find answers somewhere else. Therefore, make sure that you only provide high-quality posts regardless whether you lock your contents or not.

E-mail List

Building your email list is also an important part of a successful blog. An email list will allow you to send emails to your subscribers, as well as update your subscribers of any new posts on your blog. But, the usual problem is how you can convince people to subscribe to your email list. The way to do this is to make your readers trust you and your blog. Of course, the way to do this is by providing your visitors with top-quality contents. You should offer them a professional blog with the best user experience possible.

Newsletter

A newsletter is like a newspaper. It talks about the news or latest happenings and posts on your blog. Just like an email list, you need to get the trust of your blog visitors to make them sign up for your newsletter. Take note that a newsletter is different from email marketing. Email marketing focuses more on promotional emails (profit conversion), while a newsletter gives free information with little or no promotional value. A newsletter is a good way to give updates to your subscribers and build a good relationship.

Google Adwords (optional)

Although not required, you may find using Google Adwords to be beneficial. When you use Google Adsense, ads that promote your site can be posted on the SERP. They are usually found on the first or second page of SERP. Of course, this service is not free of charge. However, the good thing about this service is that you will surely get your money's worth. The reason is that you only have to pay a small amount for every click on your advertisement. This means that if nobody clicks on your ad and it is merely seen (page impression), then you do not have to pay anything.

Google Adwords will also allow you to choose the geographical locations where you want your ads to be visible. For example, if you only want your ads to be seen by those who reside in the United States, then you can limit the ads to that location. You can also be more specific and make your ads visible only to a particular city, like New York City and others. You can exercise full control of your advertisements. Google will also give suggestions from time to time to help you get the most of this marketing strategy. What is more, you know that this service can be trusted since it is powered by the giant of the Internet world, Google.

Paid Marketing Campaigns

There are many services online that you can find that offer to market your blog for a fee. You can find such paid campaigns on sites like Fiverr, where people post various gigs and services. It is recommended, however, that you stay away from Fiverr since most of the marketing services there are of low-quality. They will promise to send thousands of traffic to your site, but the traffic will only come from bots and fake accounts. This is not good for your SEO. In fact, Google may punish such acts. Hence, be cautious when a person or company offers to promote your blog in exchange for a small fee.

You will also find marketing campaigns that are more professional. Now, these campaigns can be effective; however, the problem is that they can be expensive. This book aims to cut down your expenses and increase your profit; therefore, it is suggested that you stay away from paid marketing campaigns. After all, if you follow the strategies and best practices in this book, you can generate a good amount of regular traffic to your blog.

Chapter 4
Blog Monetization

This chapter teaches the ways on how you can earn money with your blog. After all, with the writings and time that you dedicate to your blog, it is only fair that you get paid for your efforts. You deserve to make money with your blog.

Sell a Product or Service

This is probably the best way to earn with your blog. There are many bloggers who earn a full-time income by selling a product and service on their blog. The most common product that is sold is ebook since it is easy to make and easy to transfer to the buyer. If you decide to sell an ebook, you might want to use Amazon KDP for publishing so that your book will be sold on Amazon, which is where the great majority of ebooks are sold. However, depending on your geographical location, Amazon may not always be a good choice.

There are also many bloggers who earn a lot of money by selling their products directly on their site. There are WordPress plugins and HTML codes that you can use to make the buying and selling transactions easy and convenient. PayPal is also a good option to consider if you decide to sell something on your blog. Another site that you might want to check is Payhip.

As for selling a service, it is almost the same as selling an ebook. However, instead of selling a product, you sell a particular service, like book coaching, English tutorial, writing services, programming, and others.

Advertisements

Another effective way of earning through your blog is through ads. This time, you will post ads by other people on your blog. You can get paid either per 1,000 views or per click, or both, depending on the platform that you are using. The best ad platform to earn money from is Google Adsense. However, the problem with Adsense is that you need Google to approve your blog before it can display Google ads. The challenge here is that it is common for Google to reject an application to display Google ads. The key here is that you should only apply for Google Adsense if your blog is already established enough. This means that your blog should already have a regular flow of traffic and a good number of high-quality articles. It is recommended that you should have at least 30 articles on your blog before you apply for Google Adsense.

Take note that Google Adsense is different from Google Adwords. Adsense is when you post other people's ads on your blog so that you can earn some money, while Adwords is where you pay and create ads to promote your blog.

Affiliate Marketing

Another effective way to earn with your blog is by affiliate marketing. To be an affiliate, you need to join an affiliate program like Clickbank. You can easily find many affiliate programs online.

So, how does affiliate marketing work? When you use affiliate marketing, you promote or review a product on your blog, and when people click on your link and buy the product, you then get a profit which is usually a small part of the purchase price. Now, there are many ways to earn through affiliate marketing depending on your affiliate. Of course, the best way is the earning that you get when someone buys a product through your affiliate link. However, some programs will also allow you to earn per view or per click on your link, even if the person does not purchase the product. Again, this depends on the affiliate program that you are using.

It is noteworthy that although the goal of affiliate marketing is to be able to sell a product, you should not oversell a product just to earn a profit. A true affiliate marketer will give an honest review of a product, and this means including the disadvantages that may be associated with the product. Remember not to oversell a product. When your blog visitors realize that you only want to rip them off of their money, they will lose their trust in you and just look for another blog.

Sponsored Post

Sponsored post is usually done by established websites. It is where you promote a company product or service by posting a review about it on your blog. In a way, it is similar to an affiliate link. However, unlike an affiliate link, you can earn money with sponsored posting simply by posting a review of a product on your blog. Of course, this depends on your agreement with the one who is selling the product or service. Like affiliate marketing, you can also profit if people buy the product through the link posted on your blog.

Now, be careful about sponsored posts. One main thing that makes this different from affiliate marketing is that you are expected to give an honest review of a product. Do not forget that you already have your own followers and connections. In fact, it is the huge following of your blog that makes a seller want to have a sponsored post on your blog. Your main duty is to be true to your followers. So, keep your reviews honest at all points, and only post about products that you would personally recommend, and not just because of the money that you can make. Unfortunately, some bloggers get blinded by the offer of money and begin to promote poor-quality products. The consequence of this is that they soon lose their followers, which is not commensurate to the pay that they get from the sponsored post. Again, your main duty is to tell the facts to your followers. To earn a regular income with your blog, you need to take care of your followers.

Offer a Course

There are also bloggers who earn with their blog by turning it into a mini school or tutorial center. They do this by offering paid courses. A recommended way to do this is by dividing a particular subject into small courses so that your clients will have many options. People like having choices, so give them as many helpful courses as you can. If course, before you can do this, you need to be sure that you have sufficient mastery or expertise of the subject.

In order to persuade people to enroll and pay for a course, it is also a good idea to give them a free sample course. Make sure to make the experience helpful and wonderful, in order to convince them to continue and pay for your other courses.

Membership Area

Another way to make money with your blog is providing a membership area. This means that some parts of your blog will be open to the public, while other parts will be locked and accessible only to those who become a member. Of course, you will charge a membership fee so that you can earn money. You can make the fee to be charged annually to a member or even monthly. In the event that no payment is made upon the lapse of a given period, then the membership will be canceled automatically. You can also offer a lifetime membership fee.

When you use this strategy to earn a profit, you need to be sure that the locked items on your blog, the ones reserved for members, are worth the money that they paid. Otherwise, your paid members may think that they have been scammed or simply be disappointed. Of course, this also means that you should still make sure that the free contents on your blog, the ones open to the public, useful and informative to your readers. Otherwise, it will be hard to convince people to sign up and be a member of the site.

Sell Your Blog

This is a way to make a huge amount of money with your blog overnight. In fact, you can earn thousands of dollars. However, the consequence is also serious: You will lose your blog permanently. Sites like Flippa and Sedo are domain marketplaces where you can buy and sell websites, which means that they are also the place where you can sell your blog.

Selling a blog is not easy. Also, buyers look for blogs that are already established. You cannot expect to sell a startup blog with a little following for thousands of dollars, except maybe if you have a really good domain name — however, such is unlikely. If you decide to build and sell blogs for a profit, then this is a good way to go. Just remember that merely listing your blog on such marketplaces is not usually enough. You also need to promote that you are selling your blog. The reason is that there are countless of websites and blogs being sold on such kind of marketplace, so it would be hard to draw any attention to your blog unless you promote it.

Fiverr

There are many people who earn thousands of dollars by posting gigs on Fiverr. Fiverr is a place where you can sell gigs for at least $5. There is an additional $1 transaction fee that is charged to a buyer, so the minimum fee for a gig is $6.

You can use this platform to offer your services. Many people earn a big amount of money on Fiverr by offering a service like sharing an author's book on their blog. Yes, many book authors pay for the promotion of their books. Of course, you should only do this if the book is related to the topic of your blog. You can also offer to write a review on your blog on a specific product or service offered by a company. There are many gigs that you can come up with that makes use of your blog. It is good to join Fiverr once your blog already has a good following so that you can deliver the best quality of work to your customers on Fiverr.

Notes

Take note that many blogs do not make money right away. In fact, they do not even start with any opportunity to earn a profit. Instead, they just focus on establishing their blog first and building a quality network of connections. You may want to consider this strategy, especially if it is your first time to blog. It simply does not look nice to see a new blog with very little contents already forcing itself to sell something to its visitors. Avoid giving the impression that your blog is all about making money at your customer's cost. As mentioned in the first chapter of this book, creating value should be your priority.

Once you have established a good foundation and a regular stream of traffic to your blog, it will be easy for you to monetize your blog. Some bloggers commit the mistake of focusing on making money right away. This is wrong. You need to earn people's trust first before they will spend even a cent on your blog offers. But, once you have their trust and you have established a good network, then it will be easy for you to offer almost anything for sale on your blog. Take note, however, that building a good foundation for your blog, as well as earning the trust of your visitors take time.

Even though making money with your blog is your objective, you should only consider money as a secondary objective when you work on your blog. The truth is that the successful blogs out there are successful not because they make tons of income per month. They are successful because many people love those blogs. These blogs have become the go-to places and the authority in their respective niches. The money that they earn is the fruit of having that status and not the other way around. So, do not confuse creating a nice professional blog with a profitable blog. If your aim is to generate a steady stream of profit with your blog, then focus on establishing the name of your blog in your niche. Profit will follow once you position your blog properly in the market.

Chapter 5
Best Practices

In order to increase your chances of success, you should know the best practices commonly observed by successful bloggers. Take note that these practices should become a natural part of your blogging efforts. These are the ways to make the most out of your blog and be successful.

High-quality articles

Of course, the most important of all is to always provide high-quality articles. This advice cannot be overstated since the articles on your blog are the number one ingredient of any successful blog. Make sure that every post on your blog is informative that people will find it useful. Of course, the quality of your post is relative to the posts of your competitors. Even if you think that a particular article is already informative enough, but if your competitors provide more helpful information, then you cannot consider your article of high quality. Therefore, you should learn to consider and study the contents of your competitors.

Another characteristic of an article that is of high quality is that it is concise. Do not write 20 words when you can express the same thing in five words. Do not forget that most of the people who make a search online do not do so for mere entertainment. Most of them want to find out the answer to their question quickly. So, keep your articles clear and concise at all times.

Divide long paragraphs

According to various studies, there is a difference between reading a book and reading on a device. Reading on a computer or any device takes more effort and places more strain on the eyes. Therefore, you need to make some adjustments to increase the readability of your contents for your readers. A good rule of thumb is to divide every long paragraph into shorter paragraphs. This will make your contents more readable. Also, people tend to avoid websites that look like big blocks of texts. So, make your contents look reader friendly and use short paragraphs that are informative, concise, and easy to understand.

Share buttons

Do not make it hard for your blog visitor to share your content. Normally, people will share an article if they find it helpful. Again, providing high-quality articles is the best way to get people to share your contents. Now, you can create and use your own share buttons. Be sure that every post that you have on your blog can be easily shared. After all, you would not know the people who would find your posts interesting. Your share buttons can be the ones provided by your blogging platform. Fortunately, these days, free sharing buttons from blogging platforms already have a nice appearance. You can, of course, still, make your own share buttons with HTML. Also, you can use services like AddThis to generate sharing buttons. The important thing is to make sure that all your posts can easily and quickly be shared, so make those buttons visible and easily accessible to your blog visitors.

Contact page

Your blog should also have a contact page so that people can easily get in touch with you. Having a contact page dissolves the barrier that isolates the blogger from his readers or visitors. It signifies that you are open to people.

Having a contact page is also essential so that people who might want to offer you something can have a way to send you a private message. For example, a particular business might want you to write a sponsored post about its product. There are many other opportunities that can open up when you have a Contact page, so be sure to have this on your blog.

You should make it easy for people to contact you. It is suggested to have a separate page on your blog for your Contact Page, and do not mix it with other contents. The Contact Page should also be positioned in such a way that it is easily visible to your blog visitors. You should also avoid using a Contact page that asks for lots of information before a blog visitor can send a message. It is good to stick the basic information only, such as a person's name and email address. Asking for more information may discourage people from sending you a message, even if willing. Always remember to make it easy and convenient for your blog visitors to contact you.

About Me page

Do not forget to include an About Me page. This page will make you appear more human and social to your readers than just a blog full of texts. It is good to include personal information and interesting stuff in your About Me page. The purpose of this page is to inform your blog readers regarding yourself as a person. Hence, feel free to mention stuff about you that are not related to your blog. This is a page where your readers can get to know more about you as a person. Feel free to share interesting information about yourself with the world.

Own a niche

Although you are free to blog about anything, you need to decide on a particular niche that your blog will be about. If your blog is too general, people may not be able to understand what your blog is really about, and so they would not even visit your site. Also, Google will find it difficult to understand just how to classify and index your site for the search engine.

If you want to achieve any success with blogging, you should have a niche. A niche is something that is more specific than just a mere theme of your blog. For example, a general blog may be a blog about writing, while a niche is a blog that is full of love poetry. Owning a niche is also the way to establish your expertise on a specific subject. Do not forget that when people make searches online, they look for experts; they want people who have mastery over a particular subject matter. Therefore, they want a blog that is focused on a certain niche.

Ideally, you should decide on your niche even before you create a blog. Take note that all the contents that you will write should be about your chosen niche, so choose your niche carefully. This is another reason why you should blog about something that you are personally interested in. If you like your topic, then you can come up with lots of contents about it no matter how specific it may be.

Take advantage of the gaps in your niche

The gaps in your niche may be your goldmine for profit. These "gaps" refer to those parts of your topic (niche) that have not yet been tackled by other bloggers or writers. Take note that just because a certain topic has not yet been written does not mean that it does not have a market. The truth is that every topic has an existing market no matter how "small" or specific that topic might be.

So, how do you discover these gaps? Well, you should know that you can create such gaps. All that you need to do is to change your perspective. Take note that many different articles can be written about the exactly the same subject. All that you need is a shift in perspective. For example, it is common to read about the benefits of drinking tea, but how about the side effects of drinking black tea before bedtime? You can then expound on this matter. You just have to squeeze and let your creative juices flow as you look at a subject from a different angle.

Google Adwords

Although not required, you can use Google Adwords to promote and send real traffic to your site. In fact, this is a better option than paying for those low-quality promotional and marketing services that promise to send thousands of traffic to your site, which are only composed of bots and fake accounts — which can hurt your blog's SEO ranking.

Use Google Plus

When it comes to drawing a good number of followers and getting more visible on Google, you may find Google Plus very useful. Google Plus is the social media platform of Google. If you think your blog posts do not get the exposure and engagements that they deserve on Facebook or Twitter, then Google Plus is the way to go.

There are many active communities in Google Plus. You can join these communities and share your blog posts with the members. Of course, you can also share your contents as Public. The good news is that you can find many active and like-minded people on Google Plus who will engage and even share your contents.

Google Plus also has a +1 feature. What it does is it recommends your content to Google. It is similar to a like button on Facebook. The more +1's you have, the more your content will be recommended to Google. The good news is that people who are active on Google Plus usually give a +1 to their connections. This platform is also a good way to get viral on the Internet, especially once you have established a good amount of quality connections. You can also find many bloggers on Google Plus who would be willing to help you promote one another's blogs.

Use white or empty spaces

Avoid making your blog look so cramped with too many contents. It is recommended that you use white or empty spaces. Your blog is similar to a house. When you enter a room and see so many things inside that are close to one another, the sight simply does not feel comfortable that it is almost difficult to breathe. In the same way, your blog should also have spaces. Let your contents "breathe."

It is important to give your blog visitors the best user experience possible. A good way to do this is to make the experience of navigating your blog easy and comfortable. Having empty spaces in your blog will not only increase the readability of your contents but will also give your blog readers a more comfortable experience.

Keep your URL short and simple

When deciding on the name of your blog, you should avoid those domain names that are hard to understand. Make sure that the name of your blog is easy to spell and pronounce. You should be able to tell someone how he can access your blog in less than three seconds, without having to explain anything. Therefore, avoid using weird spellings. Keep your URL short and simple. It must also be easy to remember.

Connect With an Influencer

Most of the people who give an advice on growing a blog would tell you to connect with an influencer. But, who is an influencer, and how do you connect with one?

An influencer is a person who is considered as an expert on a particular subject and has a good following. Therefore, they have a good "influence." So, just imagine what can happen if an influencer helps you promote even just a single post on your blog? But, how do you find an influencer?

To answer all the questions above, you first need to identify an influencer. A good way to do this, as most people recommend is by using Buzzstream. You can search for influencers on a particular subject, and you can ask for a quote. Still, the best way to connect with an influencer is through their inbox. A good tip to make your way into an influencer's inbox is by using LinkedIn. Yes, that social media platform for professionals. Many influencers are active on LinkedIn. The good news is that it is very easy to connect with influencers on LinkedIn. Once an influencer accepts your request to connect, you can then send a message to an influencer, and you can rest for sure that it will go straight into his inbox. Just be sure to send a decent and compelling message so that an influencer will not be able to ignore it.

Comment and connect

In the online world, especially in social media, people usually treat other people the way they are treated. Hence, if you make it a habit of commenting on another person's posts, you will soon see some comments rolling in on your own posts. By being kind and friendly, you can soon establish a huge amount of quality connections online.

When you write a comment, do not be like the others who obviously comment just so the other person will comment back on his work. Such is considered a bad and pathetic practice. The right way to do this is by writing an honestly. Also, do not just use a single liner. People will know exactly if you mean your comment or not. Avoid comments like "This is beautiful." or "Great." There is almost no sincerity in such. Instead, write a compelling comment. It does not have to be long but it should say something substantial and not just praise an article.

A good way to assure a person that you really read his article is by including in your comment the lines that you liked the most in his article. You can also share your own insights but do so only sparingly.

You should also avoid the practice of other bloggers who seem to get the spotlight away from the author of the article. Some people write a comment that is almost as long as the article. If you think that you have a better insight, then write an article on your blog. Remember to respect the person whose work you're commenting on, and do not ever attempt to steal away attention. Be polite and respectful at all times.

Create another blog

It is not surprising for bloggers to only achieve success on their fifth or seventh (or more) blog. Blogging takes practice. The more you blog, the better you will get. If you think that you have more time in your hands or if you simply think that your present blog has no way of getting where you want it to be, then you are always free to start a new blog. This time, you will have more knowledge and experience. You can also use your old blog to help promote the new one.

You do not have to abandon your own blog. Some bloggers manage multiple blogs at the same time. If you want, and if you think you can, then you are free to do so. Just be sure not to sacrifice the quality of your work.

Stay inspired

Inspiration can get you a long way. Especially when things are not working out the way you expect them to be, inspiration can help you stay strong and do better. Therefore, it is important to remain inspired and to keep the inspiration alive.

A good way to get inspiration is by reading about the lives of successful bloggers. Many of these top bloggers also faced challenges before they were able to build their blog empire. There are also many people who share tips and stories about their own experiences as a blogger. It is also good to connect with other bloggers from time to time and chat with them. The important thing is for you not to let the flame of inspiration to disappear. It is also easier to come up with high-quality contents with an inspired mind.

Approach it professionally

Those who blog as a mere hobby usually get what they deserve. This means they also earn either a few pennies or nothing at all. If you are serious about turning your blog into a goldmine, then you should be more serious and approach blogging as a profession or a business. This means that you should also impose discipline on yourself, like making sure that you update your blog with a fresh and high-quality article every week, and that you would answer every person who comments on your post.

Blogging professionally means taking obligations and responsibilities as a blogger. You do not just blog as a hobby, but as a duty, a calling, or as a profession. As such, you should also act professionally.

To achieve success, you need to work on your blog. Study your competitors and always seek for ways to improve your blog. Always strive for continuous improvement.

The top bloggers who earn a full-time income with their blog may not have to wake up early just to get to the office since their blog is now their office. However, this does not mean that they no longer exercise any discipline. In fact, they need to be more disciplined since their income now depends on their own efforts. Not to mention, the competition in the blogging industry is really tough. Considering the many blogs out there, there are also new and start-up blogs that are created every day, and some of which will be a direct competitor, even a threat to another person's blog.

When you approach blogging professionally, you also have to consider the competition. In business, your strengths and weaknesses are always relative because they depend on the strengths and weaknesses of your competitors. Therefore, you should keep your eye on your competitors. It is worth noting that competition is not bad. In fact, significant developments are discovered due to competition. Also, if you realize that a certain market has little competition, then it is usually a sign the market may not be a profitable one. Of course, this is only the general rule and is subject to a few exceptions. But, you need to embrace the competition, which leads us to the next topic.

Embrace the competition

Do not let the competition, no matter how hard it may be, discourage you from blogging. In fact, many bloggers who are in direct competition even help one another. This is how the competition in blogging may be different from the usual competition in businesses where they try to pull one another down. Blogging has a more friendly competition. In fact, when you are a start-up blog, many top bloggers may even help promote your contents on social media. After all, your "business" exists online, and sometimes all you need is for your market to click to make you earn money. Hence, strive to create a mutual gain with your competitors.

The key is not to view your competitors as competitors, but simply as people who happen to blog in the same niche as you. It is good to learn from one another. Also, what you can do is to share your followers. This is a usual blogging practice, especially on social media. You do not need to divide or rule the competition, you simply have to work with it and establish a good relationship. After all, there is no way that you can remove the competition. If there is no or only a little competition, then you might want to reconsider if it is still something that is worth pursuing.

Make your blog mobile friendly

Most people who access the Internet usually do so using their mobile phone. Of course, they still access the Internet using their laptop and desktop computers, but mobile Internet has also become a normal trend these days. Therefore, be sure that your blog can be properly accessed and viewed on a mobile phone, as well as on other devices like tablets. Do not worry; most blogging platforms will help you make your blog as available on a mobile device as it is on a desktop computer.

Link building

Link building is important, especially for SEO purposes. In fact, Google considers the number of sites that link to your blog as another major factor of your blog's SEO ranking. The more sites link to your blog, the higher SEO ranking you will get. But, how do you get these sites to link to your blog? Again, you need to go back to the basics, such as providing high-quality contents and improving the overall appearance and features of your blog.

Mastery over your niche is also an important part of link building. If people see that you know your niche well through the articles that you publish, then they may use your blog as a reference (link).

It is worth noting that link building is not just about getting other sites to link to your blog. It is also recommended that you link to other well-established sites or blogs. This is true especially if you want to establish credibility in your articles. By linking to a well-established site or blog, your readers can check the references themselves and verify the truthfulness of your article or your conclusion.

If you are active on social media and connect with other bloggers, it is also common for bloggers to help one another by linking articles with one another's blogs. But, of course, you should only do this if the blog that you are linking to can be trusted and has good contents.

Establish trust

One thing that is common about highly successful blogs is that they are trusted by so many people. In the online world where it is easy to cheat and hide your true identity, people are cautious of who they deal with. This is another challenge that you face as a blogger. Considering such disadvantage, you still need to convince people to trust you and your blog. So, how do you do it?

Making people to trust you in an online setup is not something that you can impose. Rather, it is something that you earn. However, you do not earn it by demanding it. Instead, you have to work on it by offering the top and freshest contents to your readers. If your blog is able to help people, then these people may trust you in return. The thing here is that you do not really focus on getting any trust from your readers. Rather, you just have to focus on building the best blog that you can ever make.

Once you earn the trust of your readers, then you have to take good care of it. Take note that your responsibility as a professional blogger does not end. Do not worry; if you are truly devoted to your blog, then these things would not be a problem. This is another reason why it is strongly advised that you blog about something that you are personally passionate about. Otherwise, you would easily get tired of working on your blog.

Just as there is no secret to earning the trust of your blog visitors, there is also no secret on how you can maintain a good trust rating. You simply have to continue what you have been doing and stick to the best practices. Faithfully work on your blog with good intentions, and trust will follow.

Take a break

Building a profitable and successful blog takes time. You should give your blog a few months, at least four months, up to a year, before you can see a significant amount of profits rolling in. Of course, if you are lucky, then you might earn a huge amount of income even within the first week, especially if you have a huge following. People usually hit a quick success by selling a high-quality ebook on their blog. But, in the real world, although such quick gains are possible, there is a higher probability that you will not earn anything in the first month. It is the time for building a foundation. It is wrong to advise beginners to focus on profits right away. The first few months of blogging should be focused on building a good foundation, which includes establishing a reader base and quality connections or followers.

Regardless whether you have a new blog or a blog that is already established in its niche, you should learn to take a break from time to time. You should view a blog as an investment and not a quick way to make money from. It is also common for new blogs not to get enough exposure. Hence, it is normal for high-quality articles only to get a good number of readers only months after it is published. Building a blog empire takes time, just as building a good number of active followers on social media also takes time. This is because apart from producing high-quality contents, you also need to build good relationships. Again, you need to build trust. These things are not easy to make, and they always take time. Therefore, take a break from time to time, and do not rush the development of your blog. Do not forget that by allowing yourself to rest, you will be able to blog more effectively.

Have an established routine

Okay, people usually shy away from routines. But, take note that running a successful blog is about observing the same best practices over and over again. For example, before you can even make a new post, you need to either research the topic or simply share what you know. You then have to let it pass some rounds of editing, and then you need to proofread your work prior to publishing. And, do not forget to include an image (optional). After publishing, you need to make sure that the published piece follows the right layout, and that the spacing is correct. Next, take the time to share your new post via social media. Within a few minutes, you can expect to see comments rolling in, and then you have to reply to all these comments. This is a simple routine that most bloggers go through. As it appears, there is no step in this basic routine that you can sacrifice because it involves the required steps that you need to publish a new blog post with a simple promotional effort via social media. You also need to take some time to build a good network of connections and take care of your connections. Also, do not forget to write insightful comments on other people's posts.

Chapter 6
Common Pitfalls

Success in blogging does not just mean doing the right thing but also requires that you avoid certain pitfalls that can ruin your success. Therefore, it is important for you to be aware of the common mistakes that beginners make so that you can prepare and make the necessary adjustments and not commit the same mistakes.

Plagiarism

Plagiarism is rampant online. There are many bloggers who engage in rewriting other people's contents. Take note that Google does not like duplicate contents, and duplicate contents do not just refer to articles that are written in the same words, but also to those articles that say the same things even if written using different words. If you want to have a successful blog, then it is important for you to focus on uniqueness.

It is unfortunate that some people think that since a particular article has passed Copyscape or other plagiarism checkers online, it already means that the article is free from plagiarism. This is not correct. Take note that plagiarism includes any act where you claim another person's idea as your own. Hence, even if your article is written using different words and passes Copyscape, it does not always mean that it is already free of plagiarism.

In order to avoid plagiarism, you should learn to cite your sources or references. To do this, you can follow the APA or

MLA formatting. There are many websites online that will teach you how to use such formatting. However, if you find the instructions difficult to follow, you can just use your own way of citing your references. Just be sure to cite all your sources, and do not claim them as your own.

Of course, the best way to avoid plagiarism is by sharing your own unique ideas. Be sure that when you cite something that is not common knowledge or comes from another person, always cite your source clearly. Also, although it is good to use Copyscape or any other plagiarism checker, it is not good to rely on them completely.

Buying visitors and followers

Highly successful blogs usually have a huge number of followers and blog visitors. Sometimes, as a blogger, you cannot help but desire to reach this level quickly. When you make a search online, you will find services that offer to send a huge traffic and even followers to your blog. At first, you may think this is an excellent idea. After all, when people see that you have lots of followers, then they will think that your blog is trustworthy and reliable, correct? No. Such is a wrong way of thinking. In fact, it is not suggested that you buy blog visitors and followers. Not only will it cost you money but it can also be harmful to your blog's SEO ranking.

The problem with buying visitors and followers is that you will only be buying low-quality traffic and followers. These are the connections and visitors coming from fake and bot accounts.

Imagine visiting a site with thousands of followers but with little or no engagements in the articles, would you still think that it is a reliable blog? Of course not. Because you know that the followers are fake. You know that the owner of the blog is manipulating what you see when you visit the blog. Not to mention, such practice of buying followers and blog visitors looks so pathetic.

Low-quality traffic is bad for SEO reasons, and having low-quality followers is completely useless. Take note that people do not trust a blog based on the number of followers a blog has. Instead, people trust a blog because they like the contents or articles posted on the blog. Therefore, instead of wasting your time and money with low-quality followers and visitors, you should spend more time and effort in creating high-quality blog posts.

There are also services today that will not just give you followers, but these followers will also engage on every post that you make. At first, this may look convincing, especially if your blog lacks engagements. However, the problem here remains the same. Those followers are still of low quality and cannot truly engage on your articles, simply because they cannot give you responsive answers once you reply to their engagements. This is problematic and even embarrassing since other people will easily be able to tell that you have only bought your followers, and worse, even the engagements on your blog.

Remember: You do not buy followers. You should earn them by providing value to your blog visitors. Again, do not rush the development of your blog. Just stick to the best practice and continue to provide quality contents, and those followers and blog visitors will come. The good news is that they will be of high quality composed of active people who can really help your blog succeed. And, what is more, you do not need to waste your money.

Too much time with promotions

This is a common mistake that even veteran bloggers are still quite guilty of. Promoting your blog, especially via social media, can be addicting. However, no matter how tempting it can be to spend hours promoting your stuff on social media and seeing an increase in your blog's traffic, you should control how much time you put in your promotion. This does not mean that promotion is not important, but you need to limit how much time you invest in promotion. It is not surprising to see bloggers who spend more time with promotion than creating new posts for their blog. This is not a good practice. Do not forget that your main responsibility is as a blogger, and not as a promoter. And, as a blogger, you need to produce high-quality blog posts regularly. Therefore, even though promotion is a vital part of blogging, make sure to keep it under control and place more focus on producing top-quality blog posts.

Not using ALT text on images

Using images is good. In fact, it is recommended that every post that you make on your blog should be accompanied by at least one image. After all, it is not nice to see a post that is nothing but a big block of texts. However, if you just add an image, even if it is closely related to the keywords of your article, Google, and other search engines will not be able to recognize it. To make search engines like Google understand what your image is, you need to add ALT texts. Take note that search engines do not understand images. They need to read something in text format.

ALT texts refer to the short description that you usually see below an image. They usually tell what the image is. In fact, these texts tell the search engine what the image is about. To further improve your blog post's SEO, you can use your article's keywords as part of your ALT texts.

Expecting for quick results

As already stated, blogging takes time. Especially for new and start-up blogs, it is wrong to expect to get any result quickly. In fact, even after uploading a high-quality article on your blog, there is no assurance that it will immediately receive the exposure and attention that it deserves. Hence, do not expect any quick result. Instead, focus your attention on adding more helpful contents on your blog.

You should set small goals. For example, aim to increase your number of followers by 5% this week. Do not forget that a grand success is composed of many small successes.

Not editing your articles

This is an important part of any process of creating content for your blog. Make sure that you edit your articles properly before and even after publication. Prior to publishing your article, it is a good practice to edit your manuscript at least twice.

The proper way to edit an article is by editing it at different times of the day. It is not good to edit an article right after writing it unless you also intend to give it another round of editing at a different time. This is true, especially if you do not have anyone else to edit your article for you. The thing is that, when it comes to editing, you need to look at and examine your article with fresh eyes and a clear mind. Also, you should not rush the editing process. You do not want to ruin the quality of your article with simple grammar errors that you simply overlooked.

Not responding to comments

As you continue to blog, you will soon be on a level where people will comment on every new post that you make. Once you reach this level, remember to take the time to respond to every comment. So, should you reply literally too all comments on your post? Ideally, yes, you should try to reply to all those comments as much as you can. Take into consideration that these people take the time and effort to comment on your post, it is only fair and just for you to take some time and effort to respond to their comments. This is also the way to build a good rapport with your readers. If these people are also bloggers like yourself, then you might also want to check their blog and write an honest comment. Again, in the Internet world, you usually get the same treatment as the way that you treat other people.

Of course, when you respond to a comment, you should not forget to thank your reader for commenting, especially when you receive a helpful and insightful comment. Now, there may also come a time when you will receive a negative comment. When you receive a negative or bad comment, there are two things that you can do: You can reply back or you can simply ignore the comment. However, before you react to a bad comment, it is recommended that you first analyze and find out if the negative comment is reasonable. If it is reasonable, then you should be kind and open enough to make the necessary adjustments, and even thank the one who commented for giving you a good suggestion to make your blog better. However, if it appears that the comment was made without any good basis and simply for the purpose of writing something offensive, then you can either reply politely or simply ignore the comment. Between the two, it is recommended that you just ignore it. Take note that no matter how rude a comment may be, you should maintain your composure and professionalism. After all, if the said negative comment is completely unreasonable, your other followers will recognize it. It fact, they might even be the one who will defend your blog against the one who wrote the negative comment.

Not using a call to action message

It is worth noting that most people who search for answers online are open to suggestions. In fact, this is obvious since the reason why they look for blogs or websites online is to learn the opinions of other people. This makes them more open to suggestions — which is something that you should take advantage of. Therefore, do not forget to include a call to action message. A call to action is a message that suggests to your readers what to do next.

A call to action message is usually placed right after the article. The reason is that you first need to convince your reader to listen to you. To do that, he must first read and like your high-quality article. Now, right after reading your article, you can then insert your call to action message. Remember to keep your message short and simple. It is a good practice to limit it to just one or two sentences. Of course, you should use a hyperlink to lead your reader to the next action.

It is helpful to use a call to action message to offer a product or service to your readers. It can also be a way to suggest another page on your site that you think would be helpful to your reader. In an article, it is common to use even up to three inbound links. However, sometimes, you need to guide your readers as to the best article that he should read next. For example, if your article is about making money with advertisements posted on your blog, then a call to action to read your article about Google Adsense may be the best suggestion that you can make. Having a call to action message is one of the best things that you should have on your blog. Use it wisely.

Conclusion

Thanks for making it through to the end of this book. We hope it was informative and able to provide you with all of the tools you need to achieve your goals whatever they may be.

The next step is to apply everything that you have learned. So, it is time for you to create a blog, develop it, and earn a regular stream of profits. After all, the best way to learn how to blog is still through actual practice.

By now, you should already have a good understanding of blogging, as well as your responsibilities as a professional blogger. Blogging is a journey, and there are so many things that can happen when you blog. Do not forget that blogging is not just about making money. It can also change lives – even your own. Enjoy the experience and give it your best. This is your chance to share what is meaningful in your heart with the world. Make it count.

Finally, if you found this book useful in any way, a review on Amazon is always appreciated!

www.ingramcontent.com/pod-product-compliance
Lightning Source LLC
Chambersburg PA
CBHW071235220526
45468CB00002B/870